HOMEMADE
DOG TREATS
USING BAKING MATS
2 IN 1 GUIDE + COOKBOOK

Cook up Love and Health for Your Pooch. Irresistible Homemade Dog Treats and Meals for Oven-Safe Delights. Pamper Your Pup with Flavorful, Nutritious Recipes!

Sophia Vance

TABLE OF CONTENTS

Introduction 7

Chapter 1: **Baking Mats For Pets-Delicious!**................ 8

Chapter 2: **Preparation Is the Key Element** 10

The Utensils...11

The Baking Mat... 12

Choice of Ingredients 14

Safe foods... 14

Forbidden Foods 15

Chapter 3: **Nutritional Guidelines**........................... 17

Proteins 18

Carbohydrates... 18

Fats 18

Vitamins and Minerals..................................... 19

Fiber 20

Water 20

Feeding Guide..20

Testimonials 21

Chapter 4: Tips and Tricks for Storing Treats 22

Store the Food Under Cool, Dark, and Dry Conditions....................23

Clean the Storage Containers..23

Use Appropriate Containers and Food Storage Methods................23

Use Natural Preservatives...24

Cool the Treats Before You Store Them.......................................24

Store Wet Foods and Dry Foods Separately..................................24

A Vacuum Sealer is Helpful 25

Chapter 5: Imperial/Metric Conversion Chart...........26

Dry Ingredients..26

Liquids 27

Oven Temperatures 28

Chapter 6: Dog Biscuits and Chews 29

Pumpkin Flaxseed Dog Biscuits...29

No Flea Dog Biscuits..31

Vegan Dog Biscuits 33

Doggie Breakfast Biscuits 35

Himalayan Dog Chews...37

Chapter 7: Dog-Nuts, Pup-Tarts, and Pup pies...........39

Banana Donuts 39

Apple Donuts 41

Pup-Tarts...42

Valentine's Tarts 44

Pumpkin Pie 45

Peanut Butter Pie 47

Chapter 8: Dog Treat Recipes 49

Cottage Cheese Treats 49

Peanut Butter Dog Treats 51

Cheese Dog Treats 52

Meaty Treats 54

Meat and Cheese Dog Treats 55

Tuna and Pumpkin Dots 57

Peanut Butter Mini Dog Treats 58

Herby Tuna Treats 60

Liver Treats 61

Sweet Potato and Banana "Barkies" 63

Multi-Grain Peanut Butter Dog Treats 65

Apple and Carrot Cookies 67

Banana Bread Soft Chew Dog Treat 69

Blueberry, Oats, and Peanut Butter Treats 71

Cranberry Cookies 73

Milk Cookies 74

Vegan Dog Treats 76

Chicken Dog Treats 78

Canine Cookies 79

Pumpkin Apple Treats 80

Sweet Potato Dog Treats 82

Spinach, Carrot, and Zucchini Dog Treats 84

Vanilla Yogurt Cookies 86

Fennel Dog Treats..87

Doggie Breath Mints 88

Chapter 9: Cookies and Treats for Dogs with Health Issues **90**

Apple Peanut Butter Treats for Diabetic Dogs 90

Dog Treats for Sensitive Stomach 92

Dog Treat for Dogs With Kidney Disease.................................93

Banana Almond Dog Treats 95

Conclusion **97**

References **98**

Image References...98

INTRODUCTION

Are you looking for delicious recipes to make dog treats using baking mats? Do you want to know how to care for your dog's health by making healthy treats using the best ingredients? Do you want to avoid giving your dog commercial foods containing harmful preservatives and other additives? Then this dog treats recipe book is just what you have been looking for.

If you have some baking mats, you can make a whole range of dog treats for your pet. Everything from meat and fish to vegetables and fruits can be used for baking dog treats using these mats. They are easy to use, and you can make a few batches at a time without much of a hassle. This recipe book will tell you exactly why you must switch from commercial dog treats to homemade ones. It will also tell you how to do it most simply and conveniently while having fun with many recipes.

Commercial dog treats may seem convenient, but you never know what ingredients are used in them. Feeding your dog something with unhealthy ingredients and preservatives will negatively affect their health in the short and long term. If your dog has health issues, it becomes even more important to consciously feed them homemade treats that nourish them back to health. With this book, you will be able to achieve this.

While homemade food is very healthy, it can be dangerous if you don't follow some guidelines for pets. Pet poisoning is far more common than you believe and can occur due to the most common household ingredients. The book contains a simple list of foods to avoid and foods safe and recommended for dogs. This can guide you when making new treats for your furry buddy.

Practicing good hygiene and properly storing homemade food will make a lot of difference in avoiding mishaps. The book contains delicious recipes to make the best treats for your favorite furry friend. They include all the healthiest ingredients considering what is good for your dog and what isn't. While you have fun trying new recipes, you can add a lot of variation to your diet with each new treat. Just like humans, dogs will benefit from a diet filled with different ingredients instead of being fed the same commercial dog food daily. You can also use these recipes to try out your own new versions. So, if you're ready to start using those baking mats, read this book and get baking!

CHAPTER 1:

BAKING MATS FOR PETS-DELICIOUS!

Treats are one of the easiest tools to use when training your dog, but they are also something that you want to spoil them with just because of how great they are. However, if you buy commercial dog treats, they are highly processed and contain empty calories.

Processed kibble and dog treats provide dogs with very little nutrition. Instead, they contain many harmful preservatives, sugars, oils, etc. If you look at the labels, you may assume that they contain every nutrient necessary and are an easier choice than cooking for your dog. Most food production methods occur at high temperatures that kill many of the natural nutrients in the food. This is why commercial dog food barely gives your dog the nutrition he/she needs to stay healthy, even if the label says otherwise.

Even the protein substitutes in commercial dog food are harmful. These proteins are not obtained from natural animal sources and are difficult for your dog to digest. This, in turn, leads to the development of dietary intolerances. Providing your dog with natural proteins from meat or fish ensures easy digestion and good health.

This is why choosing natural ingredients and making homemade food for them is important. This way, you know exactly what you are feeding your dog and don't have to worry about the effects of hidden ingredients or the lack of nutrition from commercial products. The simplest way to make healthy homemade treats for your dog is with baking mats. They make it extremely easy for you to bake batches of small treats you can give your dog any time. These mats are made specifically to prepare treats for your pets, and you won't have to deal with the hassle of using cutters to make kibble-sized treats or some complicated process. After pouring the batter into/over the baking mat, you must follow the recipes and bake the treats in your oven.

So, stop buying commercial dog food or treats from here on. The only healthy alternative is to make your dog treats yourself, and with the baking mat recipes in this book, you'll ace it!

CHAPTER 2:
PREPARATION IS THE KEY ELEMENT

Preparation is key when you want to cook or bake anything for yourself and your dog. Baking homemade treats will be a hurdle if you don't have the right tools and ingredients in your kitchen. It doesn't mean you have to spend a ton of money on expensive, fancy gadgets or tools you can't afford.

You can get almost any quality baking equipment at a decent price. It is worth the investment if you use these tools multiple times over the years. Most of them will be useful for home baking for yourself and your family and do not need to be used solely for your dog.

THE UTENSILS

- Melting pot: While the double boiler method is effective, melting certain ingredients in a melting pot is much easier.

- **Mixer:** A kitchen aid mixer will make it easy to mix ingredients efficiently.

- **Food processor:** A food processor is handy when you want to chop something up quickly.

- **Baking mats:** Get a couple of different sizes and shapes of baking mats for different dog treat recipes. If you don't get the right mat size for your oven, the silicone ones can always be cut into appropriate sizes.

- **Baking tray:** Baking mats should not be placed directly on the oven floor, so you can use a baking tray to place them on.

- **Baking rack:** When you place the baking mat into the oven, you can place it on the baking rack before closing it.

- **Squeeze bottles:** Pouring the batter into a squeeze bottle will make pouring into the small molds in your baking mats easy. Using spoons or spatulas will usually be messy and cause wastage.

- **Spatulas:** A spatula is a must-have for mixing batter. You can buy a stainless steel or a silicone one if you prefer something flexible.

- **Measuring spoons and cups:** Always use accurate measurements when following baking recipes if you want the ideal results. You will need a nice set of measuring spoons and cups in your kitchen to do this.

- **Wood rolling pin:** Use a clean wood rolling pin to roll out your cookie batter when you want.

- **Wax paper:** Wax paper is useful when rolling out the treats or wrapping and storing them.

- **Cooling rack:** A cooling rack should let the treats cool completely on the baking mat once you remove them from the oven. Treats should never be stored in containers until they have cooled down completely.

- **Whisk:** A whisk is one of every home baker's most basic baking tools. You will want a good whisk to help you eliminate any clumps or lumps from your batter.

- **Airtight containers:** Airtight containers are essential to ensure that the treats you bake stay fresh and edible for longer. While dry treats will stay fresh in normal containers, other treats must be stored in airtight containers. A lot has been explained about properly storing your baked dog treats after this section in the book.

- **Labels:** When you bake homemade treats, they will have a shorter shelf life. It is best to mark the baking date and expected expiry date on the containers you store each batch in. The labels will also be useful when you simultaneously bake different types of treats.

- **Dehydrator:** A dehydrator is very useful when you want to make a lot of treats at once and dehydrate them to extend their shelf life. While an oven will do the job, a dehydrator will make your life easier. You can find affordable dehydrators in different sizes depending on the amount of use you intend to get out of it.

THE BAKING MAT

Baking mats are available in many varieties for making those delicious dog treats. They are usually made of silicone, and you need to check for food-grade, non-toxic ones. Also, check if the mat is meant for baking or ice cubes. You cannot use ice cube mats for baking since they are not heat-resistant. These mats have different mold shapes, and you can pick the type you prefer or feel your dog would enjoy. You will find everything from the shape of bones and fish to stars and hearts. They are a lot of fun to work with and make the treats more special for your dog.

When choosing the shape or size of the baking mold, it depends on what breed or age your dog is. It would also depend on the purpose of the food you are baking. Pick smaller shapes if you intend to use the dog treats during the training period. If the dog is small, opt for a smaller baking mold.

If your dog is a bigger size, use slightly larger mats. It is better to have a couple of different baking mats with you to use them as required. The batter from most recipes will be more than what you can fit into a single baking mat. It might be easier to have multiple mats to bake them simultaneously instead of doing it one batch at a time. Different-shaped molds will also make it easy to differentiate the type of treats you make at once.

It is easy to pour batter into the baking mats using squeeze bottles or dough scrapers. A good baking mat will be non-stick and easy to remove the treats from after baking. The non-stick surface will help you avoid using butter, cooking spray, etc., unless necessary. They are also quite easy to clean once the job is done. Another thing to remember is that these silicone mats should never be placed directly on the floor of your oven. Place them on a baking rack or onto a baking tray before turning the oven on.

CHOICE OF INGREDIENTS

The right ingredients make a lot of difference when cooking healthy treats for your dog. Not everything healthy for humans can be given to dogs. Certain foods are very toxic and cause them a lot of harm. The following lists will help you shop for healthy ingredients before baking for your dog. You will also learn about foods you must avoid to prevent health issues.

Safe foods

• *Apple flesh without seeds or cores*	• *Oranges in small amounts*
• *Banana*	• *Blueberries*
• *Mango*	• *Cantaloupe*
• *Pineapple*	• *Peach*
• *Watermelon*	• *Celery*
• *Cucumber*	• *Carrots*
• *Cheese in moderation*	• *Eggs*
• *Peanuts*	• *Cashews*
• *Popcorn or Corn*	• *Honey*
• *Coconut*	• *Fish like salmon and sardines*
• *Shrimp*	• *Wheat*
• *Quinoa*	• *Grains*
• *Green beans*	• *Raspberries*
• *Strawberries*	• *Brussel sprouts*
• *Peas*	

Forbidden Foods

A lot of people assume that any food safe for humans is safe for dogs. However, this is not true, and a lot of those foods can be toxic for your dog. While alcohol and tobacco are some obvious things to avoid, you might be surprised by foods like broccoli that are actually on the forbidden food list for dogs.

• **Alcohol**	• **Apricot**
• **Cherry**	• **Apple cores or seeds**
• **Plum seeds**	• **Avocado**
• **Coffee**	• **Chicken or turkey skin**
• **Ham**	• **Turkey bones**
• **Grapes**	• **Raisins**
• **Almonds**	• **Pistachios**
• **Macadamia nuts**	• **Mushrooms**
• **Nutmeg**	• **Cinnamon**
• **Ice cream**	• **Onions**
• **Garlic**	• **Chives**
• **Salt**	• **Tomatoes**
• **Raw potatoes**	• **Sugar-free gum**
• **Candy**	• **Tobacco**
• **Raw dough**	• **Yeast**
• **Raw meat**	• **Tea**

If your dog eats toxic food, get help as soon as possible. Don't try to figure it out yourself; go to a vet instead. Look for signs of distress, bloody stool, vomiting, or pain. You may even check if their stomach feels hard due to bloating from gas. If you notice any such symptoms, your dog needs help. The sooner they are treated, the easier it will be to eliminate the toxins. However, your dog should be able to avoid such issues if you keep any toxic foods out of their reach. Use the list of foods to avoid to figure out what you shouldn't be feeding your dog.

Pay attention to whether your dog is overweight or underweight. While healthy eating is important, the portions matter too. If you can see their pelvic bones or ribs and not much fat on their bones, your dog is probably underweight. Look out for loss of any muscle mass. Underfed dogs will be very susceptible to infections, have stunted growth, and won't be able to nurse their young puppies. They may even develop osteoporosis.

On the other hand, if you can't feel their ribs because of too much fat and their waist is not discernable, your dog may be overweight. Most adult dogs tend to be obese when they are fed overenthusiastically. This can lead to osteoarthritis and diabetes. Ideally, if your dog is a healthy weight, you will be able to notice an abdominal tuck and feel their ribs when probed. Look out for weight issues in dogs since you are responsible for keeping them at an ideal weight as much as possible.

Another point some dog owners ignore is that dogs should be fed at the same time every day and given the same amount of food. This will regulate their eating habits as well as their digestion. Avoid giving them table scraps, even if they sit there begging for some. Overfeeding your dog or feeding them at random times will strain their system and affect them negatively.

If you make dog treats with safe ingredients and follow a few feeding guidelines, your canine friend can grow healthy and live long.

CHAPTER 3:
NUTRITIONAL GUIDELINES

How much do I feed my dog? How much do they need, and how much is too much? What should they be eating? Every good dog owner has these questions running through their mind. A dog's health and happiness are directly related to their food, and paying attention to their diet is important.

Dogs need a healthy balance of carbohydrates, proteins, fats, fiber, vitamins, and minerals to live a long, happy life. A healthy gut directly impacts how happy or relaxed your dog will be. However, the exact nutritional requirements may vary according to your dog's breed, age, and size. Consulting your vet for nutritional guidelines will prove very helpful. In the meantime, you can learn basic nutritional information to help keep your dog well-fed and healthy.

A large portion of your dog's diet should include meat, but they also need plant matter. Being omnivores, they can digest both kinds of food well. At least two-thirds of their daily diet should consist of meat-based food. The rest should be a good balance of all the other essential nutrients that their bodies need.

PROTEINS

Dogs need a good amount of dietary protein throughout their lives. They need about 10 amino acids, which their bodies don't make and must be provided through food. This is especially important during their growth phase. The amount of proteins that young puppies need is almost double that of an adult dog. Since they play around a lot at a younger age, it helps provide more energy. Good sources of protein for dogs include meat, eggs, and fish. Puppies need about 56 g of daily crude protein. Adult dogs need around 25 g of protein. Pregnant dogs need about 69 g of protein, while nursing dogs need 158 g.

CARBOHYDRATES

Dogs also need a certain amount of healthy carbohydrates. These foods supply them with antioxidants, fiber, vitamins, and minerals. High-fiber carbohydrates, in particular, will benefit their gut health and bowel movements. Legumes and certain fruits and vegetables are good sources of healthy carbs for your dog. Some grains benefit them since they absorb any excess water in their colon and act as a prebiotic.

FATS

Healthy fats are also essential for good health but must be provided in moderation. Since dogs like to eat a lot, they can gain weight fast and get sick. Choosing the right kind of fats for their diet will help them maintain good skin and make their coat shiny. Good fat ingredients will also aid in brain development and reduce inflammation in their bodies. They need omega-3 and omega-6 fatty acids but cannot generate them on their own. This is why you must use ingredients that will provide these healthy oils in your diet. Fish oil, low-mercury fish, flaxseed oil, and olive oil are good sources. Fats are a very concentrated energy source for your dogs, and these healthy fats will provide essential fatty acids that their bodies don't synthesize. They are very important for cell structure, and the lack of these fatty acids manifests in ailments like impaired vision. Puppies need about 21 g of fats, while adult dogs need 14 g. Pregnant dogs need 29 g of fats, while nursing dogs need 67 g.

VITAMINS AND MINERALS

Vitamins and minerals are essential for good health for dogs, just like humans. They need Vitamins A, B, C, D, E, K, niacin, and pantothenic acid. The lack of vitamin A can result in skin lesions, low immunity, vision impairment, and motor issues. The lack of vitamin E can cause reproductive failure and even the breakdown of skeletal muscle. Riboflavin is needed for enzyme functions, and the lack of it can cause anorexia or eye lesions. Thiamin deficiency can cause lesions in the brain and even lead to death if there is a chronic deficiency. Niacin deficiency causes weight loss, inflammation, and excessive salivation. Meat, shellfish, bone, organ meat, fruits, and vegetables are all good sources of vitamins.

Minerals are needed to maintain the optimal functioning of their systems. They also improve muscle, bone, and teeth strength. Dogs need calcium, magnesium, phosphorus, iron, chlorine, potassium, sodium, copper, zinc, selenium, manganese, and iodine. The lack of calcium can cause major bone loss and skeletal abnormalities. Growing puppies need a healthy supply of minerals and vitamins for healthy development, even more than older ones.

However, some vitamins must be provided in recommended amounts since excessive dosage can be toxic. For instance, vitamin D should be given in small doses of 3.4 ug.

FIBER

Fiber is essential for gastrointestinal health and helps maintain a healthy weight. Their diet should contain at least three to five percent fiber daily. If your dog is overweight or needs to eat less, you can add more fiber to their treats to keep them feeling full. However, avoid excessive fiber in their diet since it can affect the ability of their system to absorb nutrients from other foods. It also causes something similar to diarrhea in them.

WATER

Hydration is another key element to keeping your dog healthy. Active dogs, in particular, need a lot of water. Ensure their bowls always have fresh and clean water to drink whenever they are thirsty. Summers, in particular, can be very hot and dehydrating for furry dogs. They are at risk of getting overheated and should have enough water available. In general, dogs need about an ounce of water per pound of their body weight daily. Even when you take your dog out for a walk or exercise, give them some water.

FEEDING GUIDE

A general guideline for feeding your dog is to give them food that is about two to three percent of their body weight. This food can be split into two or three meals a day. If your dog is overweight or inactive, they need less food. Or you can reduce their carbs and fats and increase the other nutrients. Remember that each dog is different, and their nutritional and feeding requirements will differ. Puppies should usually be fed at least two or three meals daily. Inactive adult dogs can get by with one or two meals.

Another point you may be confused about is feeding them raw or cooked food. It is best to give them cooked food since it is easier to digest and kills bacteria. Not all dogs are suited for raw feeding. The recipes here will help you make the healthiest treats for your dog while using nutritious ingredients that benefit them. However, when it comes to giving your dog a bone, always give them a raw bone. Cooked bones are dangerous because they can splinter and injure them internally, but raw bones are good to chew on and benefit dogs.

TESTIMONIALS

Testimonial #1

It's a no-brainer that home-cooked stuff is better than packaged meals, even for your dogs. My senior dog loves the occasional treats, and I have always loved making special treats for him at home. These are baked using high-quality ingredients on baking mats that are safe to use, and I only trust these for my pooch.

Testimonial #2

The idea of feeding my dog factory-produced and preservatives laced food doesn't seem right to me. I don't mind going the extra mile and cooking special treats for Bosco. He enjoys them, and I am at ease knowing he is eating nutritious yet delicious goodies.

Testimonial #3

As a vet, several pet parents ask me for suggestions on what they can feed their fur babies. Although there are quality products available in the market, I completely trust ingredients that I personally source and buy and then cook/bake them at home. Whether it is kibble or treats, homemade is always better than store-bought.

Testimonial #4

I love cooking for my loved ones, and my puppers are no exception to the rule. As a pet parent, it's my responsibility to provide my dogs with nothing but the best, and as far as that is concerned, no one can cook nutritious meals for them better than I do. I don't understand why anyone would give their pets sugary, unhealthy treats when you can absolutely make healthy treats and snacks at home.

CHAPTER 4:

TIPS AND TRICKS FOR STORING TREATS

Commercial dog treats contain preservatives or additives that help them last longer. They also tend to have a low-moisture content, which extends the shelf life of the food. However, with homemade dog treats, you must be a little more careful to keep them stored safely and use them before they spoil.

The shelf-life of homemade dog treats is very limited compared to commercial ones, but they are much healthier for your dog. The ingredients used in making the treats and the conditions under which they are stored will determine how long the food will last for safe consumption. Ideally, the fresher the food, the healthier your dog will be. However, you may not have the time to prepare treats every couple of days and may want to make a weekly batch or two. This is where safe storage comes in. The same shelf life as commercial food cannot be achieved, but a few tips and tricks will allow you to store the treats as efficiently as possible.

More importantly, just throw it out when you aren't sure about the food safety factor. You can always bake a fresh batch of treats. Giving your pets any stale or spoiled food can be quite dangerous, and it is better to throw away anything you aren't sure of.

STORE THE FOOD UNDER COOL, DARK, AND DRY CONDITIONS

These ambient conditions are ideal for extending the shelf life of homemade treats. Freezing and refrigeration are both effective in keeping the food from spoiling. The lower temperatures slow down the growth of any microorganisms and prevent them from becoming stale as fast too. Freezing is one of the best ways to store dog treats when you make a large batch. They can easily be defrosted before giving your dog the treats later. Try to keep the air exposure minimal when you store treats in the freezer since this lowers the risk of freezer burn.

CLEAN THE STORAGE CONTAINERS

Any storage containers you use for storing the treats should be cleaned thoroughly and sanitized. Also, ensure they are totally dry before you put food into them.

USE APPROPRIATE CONTAINERS AND FOOD STORAGE METHODS

If you want to store some treats in the freezer, you can use plastic containers after cleaning them. Plastic containers are difficult to completely sanitize after repeated use since scratches on the surfaces may harbor bacteria or food. Using them for freezer storage is safe since the low temperature will prevent spoilage. Use glass jars for treats you intend to store at room temperature. These are much easier to clean and safer for short-term storage.

USE NATURAL PRESERVATIVES

Vitamin E and vitamin C can be used as natural preservatives. These natural inhibitors will keep your homemade dog treats last a little longer. Mold inhibitors can also be used but are not ideal for homemade preparations.

COOL THE TREATS BEFORE YOU STORE THEM

Baked treats should always be cooled to an appropriate temperature before storage. You can use a cool-down oven or dehydrate the treats after baking. This will allow them to cool completely and lower the risk of exposure to bacteria that thrive in hotter temperatures. Even a little warmth can cause condensation if you store the treats in a box without cooling. These methods are also safer than simply keeping the treats in an open environment to cool in a kitchen.

STORE WET FOODS AND DRY FOODS SEPARATELY

Foods with higher moisture content, like soft cookies, will spoil dry foods if stored in the same container. Storing them together will affect their flavor, and the dry food will absorb moisture from the soft cookies and spoil faster.

Refrigerate treats made using fish or meat. When these foods are cooled, put them in an airtight container in the refrigerator. They can usually be served safely for five to six days if stored this way.

Uncooked dough should always be double-wrapped before you freeze it. Before using the dough, make sure it is properly defrosted.

A VACUUM SEALER IS HELPFUL

When you store dog treats in bags, vacuum sealing will be very helpful. It will reduce exposure and moisture inside the bag to prevent spoilage. Pop these vacuum-sealed dog treats in the freezer, and they can sometimes last months.

Here's a simple guide for the shelf life of different dog treats:

- Baked treats that are dry can be stored in the pantry for about a week and will last two weeks in the refrigerator. However, if they contain meat or fish, they can't be stored outside the refrigerator.

- Baked soft treats will usually stay fresh for up to five days if you keep them in airtight containers in the refrigerator.

- Dehydrated dog treats can last up to three weeks in your pantry.

- Gummy dog treats can last up to five days if kept in airtight containers in your refrigerator. Freezing them will make them last a few months.

CHAPTER 5:
IMPERIAL/METRIC CONVERSION CHART

DRY INGREDIENTS

Metric	Standard
1 g	.035 oz
100 g	3.5 oz
500 g	17.7 oz
1 kg	35 oz

Teaspoons	Tablespoons	Cups
3 tsp	1 tbsp	1/16 c
6 tsp	2 tbsp	⅛ c
12 tsp	4 tbsp	¼ c
24 tsp	8 tbsp	½ c
36 tsp	12 tbsp	¾ c
48 tsp	16 tbsp	1 c

LIQUIDS

Metric	Standard
1 ml	⅕ tsp
5 ml	1 tsp
15 ml	1 tbsp
240 ml	1 c

Fluid ounces	Cups	Pints	Quarts	Gallons
8 fl oz	1 c	½ pt	¼ qt	1/16 gal
16 fl oz	2 c	1 pt	½ qt	⅛ gal
32 fl oz	4 c	2 pt	1 qt	¼ gal
64 fl oz	8 c	4 pt	2 qt	½ gal
128 fl oz	16 c	8 pt	4 qt	1 gal

OVEN TEMPERATURES

Degrees Celsius	Degrees Fahrenheit
120 °C	250 °F
160 °C	320 °F
180 °C	350 °F
205 °C	400 °F
220 °C	425 °F

CHAPTER 6:
DOG BISCUITS AND CHEWS

🐕 PUMPKIN FLAXSEED DOG BISCUITS

Quantity Produced: 200 treats	**Nutritional Values:** 1 treat
Cooking Time: 40 minutes	*Fat: 1 g*
Preparation Time: 20 minutes	*Calories: 26*
	Carbohydrates: 4 g
	Protein: 1 g

Ingredients:

- 2 cups pumpkin puree
- ½ cup water
- 4 tablespoons brown sugar (optional)
- ½ cup flaxseeds
- 2 eggs
- 7 cups all-purpose flour
- ⅔ cup vegetable oil

Directions:

1. Preheat your oven to 350 °F. Place a baking mat on a large baking sheet with the flat side facing up.

2. Fit the stand mixer with the dough hook. Add sugar, pumpkin puree, and eggs into the mixing bowl of the stand mixer. Mix until well incorporated.

3. Add water and oil and mix until well combined. Take out half the mixture and set it aside for now.

4. Add half the flour and half the flaxseeds into the mixing bowl until well combined and you get a slightly hard dough.

5. Transfer the dough onto your countertop.

6. Now add the egg mixture that was kept aside into the mixing bowl of the stand mixer. Add remaining flour and flaxseeds and mix until well combined. You will get a slightly hard dough.

7. Roll each dough ball on a floured area on your countertop with a rolling pin until it is around 1/3 inch thick. Cut each into 100 equal-sized sticks with a pizza cutter. Place as many biscuits on the prepared baking mat without overlapping.

8. Bake in batches until the biscuits are light golden brown. These biscuits will be hard. Cool completely.

9. Store in an airtight container and refrigerate until use. When stored properly, it lasts for up to two weeks.

NO FLEA DOG BISCUITS

Quantity Produced: 60	**Nutritional Values:** 1 biscuit
Preparation Time: 25 minutes	**Calories:** *85*
Cooking Time: 30 minutes	**Fat:** *2 g*
	Carbohydrates: *7 g*
	Protein: *11 g*

Ingredients:

- 4 cups oats

- 2 ½ cups whole-wheat flour or any other flour of your choice

- 1 ½ cups water

- 2 cups powdered brewer's yeast

- 2 eggs

- 2 cups shredded cheddar cheese

Directions:

1. Preheat your oven to 350 °F. Place a large baking mat on a large baking sheet with the flat side on top.

2. Combine flour, oats, brewer's yeast, and cheese in a mixing bowl.

3. Crack the eggs into another bowl. Beat until the yolks and whites are well combined. Pour the eggs into the bowl with the flour mixture and mix until well incorporated.

4. Add a cup of water and mix well. Add remaining water only if you are not able to form into dough.

5. Dust your countertop with some flour. Place the dough on the dusted area and roll until it is about ¼ inch thick.

6. Cut the dough into biscuits using a round or bone-shaped cookie cutter. Collect the scrap dough and re-shape it into a ball if you cut the biscuits using a cookie cutter. Repeat steps five and six until all the biscuits are cut.

7. Place biscuits on the baking mat without overlapping.

8. Bake in an oven for 30 minutes or until the edges turn brown. Bake in batches.

9. Once the biscuits are browned, switch off the oven and let them cool completely in the oven.

10. Store in an airtight container and refrigerate it. It can last for up to 12–15 days.

VEGAN DOG BISCUITS

Quantity Produced:	**Nutritional Values:** Entire recipe
About 2 ¾ pounds	*Calories:* 3417
	Fat: 115.3 g
Preparation Time: 15 minutes	*Carbohydrates:* 549.1 g
Cooking Time: 15 minutes	*Protein:* 142.5 g

Ingredients:

- 2 bananas, mashed

- 2 cups rolled oats

- 2 ½ cups whole-wheat flour or any other flour you choose, like rice, amaranth, quinoa, etc.

- 1 cup peanut butter

- 1 cup applesauce

- 1 teaspoon ground cinnamon

Directions:

1. Preheat the oven to 350 °F. Place a baking mat on a baking sheet with the flat side on top.

2. Add bananas, oats, flour, peanut butter, applesauce, and cinnamon into a mixing bowl until the dough is formed.

3. Dust some flour on your countertop. Place the dough on your countertop and knead for a couple of minutes.

4. Roll the dough with a rolling pin until it is ½ inch thick.

5. Cut the dough into the desired shape using a knife or cookie cutter.

6. Spray cooking spray on a couple of large baking sheets. Use more baking sheets if required.

7. Place biscuits on the baking mats in a single layer without overlapping.

8. Bake in batches for 10–15 minutes or until the edges turn brown. Cool completely.

9. Transfer into an airtight container and refrigerate until use. These biscuits can last for about six to seven days.

DOGGIE BREAKFAST BISCUITS

Quantity Produced:
About 2 pounds

Preparation Time: 20 minutes
Cooking Time: 30 minutes

Nutritional Values: Entire recipe
Calories: 1528
Fat: 64.8 g
Carbohydrates: 194 g
Protein: 41.5 g

Ingredients:

- 3 cups brown rice flour

- 4 tablespoons bacon fat

- ½ cup shredded cheddar cheese

- 2 eggs

- 4 tablespoons ground flaxseeds

- 4 strips bacon, cooked until crisp, crumbled

- 2 medium carrots, shredded, cut into tiny pieces

- 10 tablespoons water

Directions:

1. Preheat your oven to 350 °F. Place a large baking mat on a large baking sheet with the flat side on top.

2. Combine rice flour, bacon fat, cheese, eggs, flaxseeds, bacon, carrots, and water in a mixing bowl until you get a dough.

3. Place a sheet of wax paper on your countertop. Dust it with a little flour. Place the dough on the wax paper and flatten it slightly. Dust it with a little flour. Place another sheet of wax paper on top of the dough and roll with a rolling pin until it is ¼ - ½ inch thick.

4. Cut the dough into biscuits using a round or bone-shaped cookie cutter, or cut into squares or rectangles with a knife.

5. Collect the scrap dough and re-shape it into a ball if you cut the biscuits using a cookie cutter. Repeat steps four and five until all the biscuits are cut.

6. Place biscuits on the baking sheet mat overlapping.

7. Bake for 10–15 minutes or until the edges turn brown. Bake in batches. Cool completely.

8. Transfer into an airtight container and refrigerate until use. They can last for about 15 days.

HIMALAYAN DOG CHEWS

Quantity Produced: 10 dog chews **Preparation Time:** 5 minutes **Cooking Time:** 20 minutes plus pressing time	**Nutritional Values:** 1 dog chew *Calories:* 68 *Fat:* 0 g *Carbohydrates:* 10 g *Protein:* 7 g

Ingredients:

- 2 quarts skim milk

- ½ teaspoon Himalayan salt

- ¼ cup vinegar

Directions:

1. Boil milk in a pot over medium-low heat. Keep stirring all the while.

2. Remove the pot from heat and stir in the salt and vinegar. Keep stirring gently for a couple of minutes or until the whey starts separating.

3. Now do not stir for about 15 minutes and let it rest.

4. Strain the mixture through cheesecloth into a bowl. The drained liquid is not required; you can discard it.

5. Gather the ends of the cloth and wring to remove any liquid from the cheese.

6. Place something heavy on the wrung cheesecloth to remove all the remaining moisture. Let it remain this way for four to five hours.

7. Remove the cheese from the cheesecloth and cut it into 10 pieces.

8. Preheat the oven to 150 °F. Place a baking mat on a baking sheet with the flat side on top.

9. Place the cheese pieces on the baking mat and set the timer for 40 minutes.

10. Place the baked chews on a cooling rack for 24–36 hours.

11. If the chews are dry, store them in an airtight container at room temperature for a few weeks. If you think they are not dried properly, place them in an airtight container in the refrigerator.

CHAPTER 7:
DOG-NUTS, PUP-TARTS, AND PUP PIES

BANANA DONUTS

Quantity Produced: 6 donuts	**Nutritional Values:** 1 donut
Preparation Time: 5 minutes	*Calories:* 174
Cooking Time: 20 minutes	*Fat:* 11 g
	Carbohydrates: 17 g
	Protein: 6 g

Ingredients:

For the Donuts:

- ½ cup mashed overripe bananas

- 2 tablespoons melted coconut oil

- 1 small egg at room temperature

- 2 tablespoons natural creamy peanut butter

- 1 tablespoon honey

- ¼ teaspoon baking soda

- ½ cup whole-wheat flour

For the frosting:

- 2 tablespoons natural creamy peanut butter

- ¼ cup Greek yogurt

- crushed dog biscuits (optional)

Directions:

1. Preheat your oven to 350 °F. Place a silicone baking mat with donut molds on a baking sheet with the cavity side on top.

2. Add mashed banana, coconut oil, peanut butter, and honey into a bowl and whisk until smooth.

3. Whisk in the egg. Add baking soda and flour into a bowl and mix well. Add the flour mixture to the bowl of the banana mixture and stir until just incorporated, making sure not to over-mix.

4. Spoon the batter into the donut molds and bake for 10–15 minutes. To check if the donuts are cooked, insert a toothpick in the donut and take it out. If you see any batter stuck on it (crumbs are ok), bake for a few more minutes.

5. Take out the pan and place it on your countertop for 10 minutes. Cool the donuts on a wire rack. You can store them in the freezer in an airtight container for a month if you do not frost them. You can make fresh frosting each time you serve.

6. Whisk together peanut butter and yogurt in a bowl to make the frosting. Spread the frosting on each donut. Garnish with crushed biscuits if using, and serve.

🐕 APPLE DONUTS

Quantity Produced: 5 donuts	**Nutritional Values:** For 1 donut
Preparation Time: 10 minutes	**Calories:** 157
Cooking Time: 10 minutes	**Fat:** 9 g
	Carbohydrates: 18 g
	Protein: 5 g

Ingredients:

For the donuts:

- 1 tablespoon vegetable oil or melted
- 2 ⅔ tablespoons creamy peanut butter
- 1/3 teaspoon baking powder
- 1 tablespoon vegetable oil or melted

- 1/3 cup unsweetened
- 1 tablespoon honey
- ⅔ cup whole-wheat flour

To drizzle:

- 2 teaspoons creamy peanut butter

Directions:

1. Preheat your oven to 350 °F. Place a baking mat with donut shapes on a baking sheet with the mold side facing on top.

2. Whisk together oil, applesauce, peanut butter, and honey in a mixing bowl until smooth.

3. Stir in the baking powder and flour. Spoon the batter into the donut holes and bake for 10 minutes. To check if the donuts are cooked, insert a toothpick in the

donut and take it out. If you see any batter stuck on it (crumbs are ok), bake for a few more minutes.

4. Take out the pan and place it on your countertop for 10 minutes. Remove the donuts from the molds and cool on a wire rack.

5. If the peanut butter is not pourable, you can melt it for a few seconds in the microwave. Drizzle some peanut butter on the donuts.

6. You can store them in the freezer in an airtight container for a month if you do not frost them.

🐕 PUP-TARTS

Quantity Produced: 8 pop tarts **Preparation Time:** 10 minutes **Cooking Time: 25** minutes	**Nutritional Values:** 1 pop tart *Calories:* 177 *Fat:* 7.4 g *Carbohydrates:* 21.7 g *Protein:* 7 g

Ingredients:

- 1 ¼ cups flour

- ½ cup water

- ¼ cup frozen vanilla yogurt drops

- ½ cup peanut butter

- ½ tablespoon vegetable oil

Directions:

1. Preheat the oven to 350 °F. Place a baking mat with the flat side facing up on a baking sheet.

2. Place flour, water, peanut butter, and oil into a bowl and mix until dough is formed.

3. Dust some flour on your countertop and let the dough rest for 10 minutes. Roll with a rolling pin into a thin rectangle.

4. Cut into eight equal rectangles. Crimp the edges of each rectangle. It will resemble a pop tart.

5. Place the pop tarts on the baking mat. Bake the pop tarts until golden brown, about 25 minutes.

6. Let the pop-tarts cool down. You can store them in an airtight container at room temperature for about three to four days or in the refrigerator.

7. When serving your furry baby, remove the yogurt drops from the freezer and let it melt. Drizzle the melted yogurt drops over the required number of pop tarts and chill until ready to serve.

VALENTINE'S TARTS

Quantity Produced: 12 tarts **Preparation Time:** 10 minutes **Cooking Time: 20** minutes	**Nutritional Values:** 1 tart *Calories:* 63 *Fat:* 2.9 g *Carbohydrates:*6.9 g *Protein:* 2.4 g

Ingredients:

- ½ cup chickpea flour

- 2 tablespoons applesauce

- 2 tablespoons canola oil

- ½ teaspoon vanilla extract

- 2 tablespoons peanut butter or almond butter

- 1 egg, beaten and divided

- ¼ cup brown rice flour

- 2 tablespoons water

- 12 whole strawberries, fresh or frozen

Directions:

1. Preheat the oven to 350 °F. Place a silicone muffin mold mat on a baking sheet.

2. Combine chickpea flour and brown rice flour in a bowl. Mix half the egg, applesauce, oil, and water until you get a dough.

3. Divide the dough into 12 equal parts and press one part into each muffin cup.

4. Add half the egg, peanut butter, and vanilla into a bowl and whisk until smooth.

5. Spoon the filling into the muffin cups. Lay a strawberry on its side in each cup.

6. Place the muffin mold mat in the oven and bake for about 20 minutes or until golden brown around the edges of the tarts.

7. Cool and store in an airtight container in the refrigerator. This will stay fresh for around a week.

PUMPKIN PIE

Quantity Produced: 12 mini pies	**Nutritional Values:** 1 mini pie
Preparation Time: 5 minutes	*Calories:* 59
Cooking Time: 8 minutes	*Fat:* 2.5 g
	Carbohydrates: 7.5 g
	Protein: 2.3 g

Ingredients:

- ¾ cup plus ⅛ cup oat flour

- ½ banana, mashed

- 6 tablespoons unsweetened applesauce

- 6 tablespoons unsweetened pumpkin puree

    For topping:

- low-fat plain yogurt

Directions:

1. Place a strainer lined with cheesecloth over a bowl. Add yogurt into the filter and let the liquid drain out.

2. Preheat the oven to 350 °F. Place a silicone baking mat with muffin molds on a baking sheet.

3. To make the crust: Add oat flour and applesauce into a bowl and mix until dough is formed.

4. Make 12 equal parts of the dough. Place one part in each muffin cup and press it well into the cup. Pierce holes in each crust with a fork.

5. Place the muffin pan in the oven and bake for about seven to eight minutes, until light brown. Let the crusts cool completely. You can make the crusts and keep them in an airtight container in the refrigerator. They can last for a week. You can prepare a fresh filling each time you serve your pet.

6. To make the filling: Combine banana and pumpkin puree in a bowl.

7. Fill the banana mixture into the crusts. Spoon some yogurt on top and serve.

🐕 PEANUT BUTTER PIE

Quantity Produced: 16 mini pies **Preparation Time:** 30 minutes **Cooking Time:** 40 minutes	**Nutritional Values:** 1 mini pie *Calories:* 194 *Fat:* 8 g *Carbohydrates:* 24.8 g *Protein:* 7.7 g

Ingredients:

For the filling:

- 1 cup peanut butter

- 2 large ripe bananas, mashed

For the crust:

- 1 cup unsweetened applesauce

- 3 cups oat flour

Directions:

1. Preheat the oven to 350 °F. Place a silicone muffin mold mat on a baking sheet.

2. To make the crust: Add oat flour and applesauce in a bowl and mix until a sticky dough is formed.

3. Make 16 equal parts of the dough. Place one part in each muffin cup and press it well into the cup. Pierce a few holes in each crust with a fork.

4. Place the pan in the oven and bake until golden brown.

5. Cool the crusts to room temperature. You can store the crusts in an airtight container in the refrigerator for a week. You can make a fresh filling each time you serve it to your baby.

6. To make the filling: Combine banana and peanut butter in a bowl.

7. Fill the banana mixture into the crusts and serve.

CHAPTER 8:
DOG TREAT RECIPES

COTTAGE CHEESE TREATS

Quantity Produced:	**Nutritional Values:** Entire Recipe
About 1.7–2 pounds	*Calories:* 1477
	Fat: 96.8 g
Preparation Time: 10 minutes	*Carbohydrates:* 67.3 g
Cooking Time: 35 minutes	*Protein:* 83.1 g

Ingredients:

- ¼ teaspoon salt

- 10.5 ounces of potato starch

- 6 eggs

- 14 ounces cottage cheese

- 4 tablespoons oil

Directions:

1. Preheat the oven to 350 °F.

2. Place eggs, oil, cottage cheese, and salt in a blender and blend until very smooth.

3. Blend in the potato starch. You should have a batter, just like pancake batter.

4. Place the silicone baking mat upside down so the cavity side is on top.

5. Pour the batter on the baking mat and spread it around with a spatula so that the batter fills up the cavities. Bake in batches if required. Make sure the edges around the cavities are free from the batter. So, scrape it off if necessary. Lift the baking mat and tap it lightly on the countertop to remove any air pockets.

6. Bake in a preheated oven for 20–35 minutes. Baking time varies according to the size of the cavities.

7. Let it cool for a while in the oven.

8. Cool completely on the countertop. Hold the baking mat on two opposite edges and twist the baking sheet to unmold. Invert the cookies onto a baking sheet.

9. Store in the refrigerator in an airtight container. They can last for about 12–15 days.

PEANUT BUTTER DOG TREATS

Quantity Produced: About 2 pounds **Preparation Time:** 5 minutes **Cooking Time:** 12 minutes	**Nutritional Values:** Entire Recipe *Calories:* 3229 *Fat:* 170.3 g *Carbohydrates:* 334 g *Protein:* 110 g

Ingredients:

- 4 eggs

- 1 cup peanut butter powder

- 4 tablespoons oil

- 1 cup water

- 1 cup tapioca flour

- 1 cup all-purpose flour

Directions:

1. Preheat the oven to 350 °F.

2. Blend eggs, peanut butter powder, oil, water, tapioca flour, and all-purpose flour in a blender until smooth.

3. Place the baking mat upturned on the baking sheet, with the cavity side up.

4. Pour the batter on the baking mat and spread it around with a spatula so that the batter fills up the cavities.

5. Make sure the edges around the cavities are free from the batter. So, scrape it off if necessary. Lift the baking sheet and tap it lightly on the countertop to remove any air pockets. Bake in batches if required.

6. Bake in a preheated oven for about 12 minutes or until the treats disappear from the molds. They may be a little soft.

7. Let it cool for a while in the oven.

8. Cool completely on the countertop. Hold the baking mat on two opposite edges and twist the baking sheet to unmold. Invert onto a baking sheet.

9. Store in an airtight container in the refrigerator. They can last for about two weeks.

CHEESE DOG TREATS

Quantity Produced: About 8-10 ounces	**Nutritional Values:** Entire Recipe
Preparation Time: 10 minutes	**Calories:** 1364
Cooking Time: 20 minutes	**Fat:** 60g
	Carbohydrates: 125.6 g
	Protein: 57 g

Ingredients:

- 1 cup shredded sharp cheddar cheese
- 1 cup rice flour
- 1 teaspoon sour cream
- ½ tablespoon oil
- 2 eggs
- water, as required

Directions:

1. Preheat the oven to 350 °F.

2. Place cheese in the food processor bowl and process until crumbly.

3. Transfer the cheese to a bowl. Add oil, flour, eggs, sour cream, and enough water to get a pancake-like batter.

4. Whisk until it becomes free of any lumps.

5. Place the silicone baking mat upside down on a baking sheet so the cavity side is on top.

6. Pour the batter on the baking mat and spread it around with a spatula so that the batter fills up the cavities.

7. Make sure the edges around the cavities are free from the batter. So, scrape it off if necessary. Lift the baking sheet and tap it lightly on the countertop to remove any air bubbles.

8. Bake for about 18–20 minutes.

9. Let it cool for a while in the oven.

10. Cool completely on the countertop. Hold the baking mat on two of the opposite edges and twist the baking sheet to unmold. Invert the treats onto a baking sheet.

11. Store in the refrigerator in an airtight container. They can last for about two weeks.

🐕 MEATY TREATS

Quantity Produced: About 1 pound **Preparation Time:** 10 minutes **Cooking Time:** 10 minutes	**Nutritional Values:** Entire Recipe *Calories:* 1525 *Fat:* 77g *Carbohydrates:* 56.8 g *Protein:* 139 g

Ingredients:

- 1.1 pounds ground beef or liver, tuna or heart

- 2 small eggs

- 2.6 ounces whole-wheat flour or gluten-free flour

Directions:

1. Preheat the oven to 350 °F.

2. Place meat in the blender or food processor until you get a smooth paste.

3. Blend in the eggs. Add flour and blend until smooth.

4. Place the baking mat upturned on a baking sheet, with the cavity side up.

5. Spoon the mixture into the cavities.

6. Make sure the edges around the cavities are free from the batter. Lift the baking sheet and tap it lightly on your countertop to remove any air pockets. Bake in batches if required.

7. Bake in a preheated oven for about 8–10 minutes.

8. Let it cool for a while in the oven.

9. Cool completely on the countertop. Hold the baking mat and twist it to unmold. Invert onto a baking sheet.

10. Store the treats in a freezer-safe container in the freezer. They can last for about seven days in the refrigerator.

MEAT AND CHEESE DOG TREATS

Quantity Produced: About 1.5–1.75 pounds	**Nutritional Values:** Entire Recipe **Calories:** 2162 **Fat:** 120.3g
Preparation Time: 10 minutes **Cooking Time:** 20 minutes	**Carbohydrates:** 123 g **Protein:** 145 g

Ingredients:

- 2 cups of ground meat of your choice

- 2 large eggs

- 1 cup grated cheddar cheese

- 1 cup rice flour

- 2 tablespoons olive oil

- water, as required

Directions:

1. Preheat the oven to 350 °F.

2. Place cheese in the food processor bowl and process until crumbly.

3. Transfer the cheese to a large bowl.

4. Place meat in the food processor and process until you get a smooth paste.

5. Transfer the meat paste to the bowl of cheese. Add rice flour, oil, and enough water to get a thick batter like pancake batter.

6. Place the baking mat upturned on a baking sheet, with the cavity side up.

7. Spoon the mixture into the cavities.

8. Make sure the edges around the cavities are free from the batter. Lift the baking sheet and tap it lightly on the countertop to remove any air pockets. Bake in batches if required.

9. Bake in a preheated oven for about 8–10 minutes.

10. Let it cool for a while in the oven.

11. Cool completely on the countertop. Hold the baking mat on opposite edges and twist the baking mat to unmold. Invert the treats onto a baking sheet.

12. Store the treats in a freezer-safe container in the freezer for about two months. They can last six to seven days if placed in the refrigerator.

TUNA AND PUMPKIN DOTS

Quantity Produced:	Nutritional Values: Entire Recipe
About 10–12 ounces	Calories: 610
	Fat: 11.5g
Preparation Time: 5 minutes	Carbohydrates: 26.2 g
Cooking Time: 20 minutes	Protein: 30.8 g

Ingredients:

- 2 cans (4.5 ounces each) of canned tuna in water (do not drain)

- 10.5 ounces steamed butternut squash or pumpkin cubes or puree

- 2 eggs with shells

Directions:

1. Empty the tuna cans into a blender along with the water in the cans. Add butternut squash and eggs and blend until you get a smooth and thick batter.

2. Preheat the oven to 350 °F.

3. Place the silicone baking mat upside down on a baking sheet so the cavity side is on top.

4. Pour the batter on the baking mat and spread it around with a spatula so that the batter fills up the cavities.

5. Make sure the edges around the cavities are free from the batter. So, scrape it off if necessary. Lift the baking sheet and tap it lightly on the countertop to remove any air pockets.

6. Bake in a preheated oven for about 20 minutes.

7. Hold the baking mat with oven mitts and twist it to unmold. Invert the treats onto a baking sheet. Place the baking sheet in the oven to dry out the treats. Leave the oven door very slightly open.

8. Store in an airtight container in the refrigerator. They can last for about two weeks.

PEANUT BUTTER MINI DOG TREATS

Quantity Produced:	**Nutritional Values:** Entire Recipe
About 5 ounces	*Calories:* 509
	Fat: 34.24g
Preparation Time: 5 minutes	*Carbohydrates:* 34.6 g
Cooking Time: 15 minutes	*Protein:* 28.2 g

Ingredients:

- 4 tablespoons natural peanut butter

- 1 tablespoon rice flour or tapioca flour

- 1 egg

- 3 tablespoons water

Directions:

1. Blend peanut butter, water, and eggs in a blender until well combined and free from lumps.

2. Add rice flour and blend until smooth. You need pancake-like batter, so add more water if required.

3. Preheat the oven to 375 °F.

4. Place the silicone baking mat upside down on a baking sheet so the cavity side is on top.

5. Pour the batter on the baking mat and spread it around with a spatula so that the batter fills up the cavities.

6. Make sure the edges around the cavities are free from the batter. So, scrape it off if necessary. Lift the baking sheet and tap it lightly on the countertop to remove any air pockets.

7. Bake in a preheated oven until golden brown, for about 15 minutes.

8. Hold and twist the baking mat to unmold. Invert onto a baking sheet when completely cooled. Place the treats in an airtight container. Store the container in the refrigerator. They can last for about two weeks. To make them last for two months, freeze them.

HERBY TUNA TREATS

Quantity Produced:	Nutritional Values: Entire Recipe
About 10 ounces	**Calories:** 715
	Fat: 19.8g
Preparation Time: 10 minutes	**Carbohydrates:** 92 g
Cooking Time: 20 minutes	**Protein:** 41 g

Ingredients:

- 1 can (5 ounces) tuna with its liquid

- ½ cup tapioca flour

- 1 tablespoon oil

- 1 egg

- ¼ cup all-purpose flour

- 1 teaspoon dried herbs of your choice

Directions:

1. Preheat the oven to 350 °F.

2. Blend tuna with its liquid, flour, oil, egg, and herbs until smooth. It should be like pancake batter, so add some water if required.

3. Place the silicone baking mat on a baking sheet so the cavity side is on top.

4. Pour the batter on the baking mat and spread it around with a spatula so that the batter fills up the cavities.

5. Make sure the edges around the cavities are free from the batter. So, scrape it off if necessary. Lift the baking sheet and tap it lightly on the countertop to remove any air pockets.

6. Bake in a preheated oven until golden brown, for about 15 minutes.

7. Hold the baking sheet on opposite sides and twist the baking mat to unmold. Invert onto a baking sheet when completely cooled. Place the treats in an airtight container in the refrigerator. They can last for about two weeks. They can last for about two months in the freezer.

🐕 LIVER TREATS

Quantity Produced: About 3 pounds **Preparation Time:** 15 minutes **Cooking Time:** 20 minutes	**Nutritional Values:** Entire Recipe *Calories:* 3038 *Fat:* 83.7 g *Carbohydrates:* 341 g *Protein:* 210 g

Ingredients:

• 2 pounds raw chicken liver or beef liver

• 2 eggs

• 2 tablespoons oil

• 3 ½ cups flour of your choice

• 2 teaspoons of herbs of your choice

• water, as required

Directions:

1. Preheat the oven to 350 °F.

2. Place meat liver in the food processor bowl and process until very smooth.

3. Add eggs, oil, flour, and herbs and process until well combined and free from lumps. If the mixture is very thick, add some water. You should have a batter like a pancake batter.

4. Place the baking mat upturned on a baking sheet, with the cavity side up.

5. Spoon the mixture into the cavities.

6. Make sure the edges around the cavities are free from the batter. Lift the baking sheet and tap it lightly on the countertop to remove any air pockets. Bake in batches.

7. Bake in a preheated oven for about 15–20 minutes.

8. Let it cool for a while in the oven.

9. Cool completely on the countertop. Hold the baking mat on two edges and twist the baking sheet to unmold. Invert onto a baking sheet.

10. Store in a freezer-safe container in the freezer for about two months. They can last six to seven days if placed in the refrigerator.

SWEET POTATO AND BANANA "BARKIES"

Quantity Produced: 60 cookies **Preparation Time:** 30 minutes **Cooking Time:** 25 minutes	**Nutritional Values:** 1 cookie *Calories:* 26 *Fat:* 0.5 g *Carbohydrates:* 5 g *Protein:* 1 g

Ingredients:

- 3 ½ cups old-fashioned oats divided

- 2 cups cooked sweet potato

- 1 medium banana, sliced

- 2 large eggs

Directions:

1. Preheat the oven to 350 °F.

2. Grind three cups of oats in a blender until finely powdered.

3. Add sweet potato, banana, and eggs and blend until well combined.

4. Transfer the mixture to a bowl. Add ½ cup of oats and mix well.

5. Make 60 equal portions of the dough (about 1 ½–2 tablespoons per cookie). Shape each portion into a ball.

6. Place the baking mat on a baking sheet with the flat side on top. Place the balls on the baking mat, leaving sufficient space between the dough balls. Bake in batches if they all don't fit on the mat.

7. With a fork, press each cookie until slightly flat.

8. Set the timer for 20–25 minutes and bake the cookies. These will have slightly soft centers. If you want hard cookies, bake them for another five to eight minutes.

9. Once they get cool, store the cookies in an airtight container in the refrigerator for about 12–15 days or in the freezer for about two months.

MULTI-GRAIN PEANUT BUTTER DOG TREATS

Quantity Produced: 9 treats **Preparation Time:** 15 minutes **Cooking Time:** 30 minutes	**Nutritional Values:** 1 treat *Calories:* 163 *Fat:* 10.2 g *Carbohydrates:* 15.7 g *Protein:* 4.9 g

Ingredients:

- ¼ cup rolled oats

- 1 cup whole-wheat flour

- ¼ cup wheat germ

- 1 tablespoon nutritional yeast

- ½ tablespoon ground flax seeds

- ½ teaspoon brewer's yeast

- ½ tablespoon whole flax seeds

- 1 tablespoon sunflower seeds

- ¼ teaspoon Himalayan salt

- 3 tablespoons creamy peanut butter

- ½ tablespoon blackstrap molasses

- ½ cup bone broth

- ¼ cup virgin olive oil

Directions:

1. Preheat the oven to 350 °F.

2. Place the baking mat on a baking sheet with the flat side on top.

3. Combine oats, salt, flour, wheat germ, nutritional yeast, brewer's yeast, sunflower seeds, ground, and whole flax seeds in a bowl. Mix well so that the salt is well distributed.

4. Stir in the peanut butter, oil, and molasses. Mix until crumbly.

5. Add bone broth and mix with your hand until you get a soft dough.

6. Dust some flour on your countertop. Place the dough on your countertop and knead for a couple of minutes.

7. Using a rolling pin, roll the dough until it's about ¼ inch thick.

8. Cut the rolled dough into the desired shape with a cookie cutter. Gather the scrap dough and re-shape it into a dough. Repeat this process on the remaining dough. You should have nine treats.

9. Place the treats on the baking mat.

10. Bake for 25 minutes or until the edges begin to turn brown. Allow it to cool completely.

11. Refrigerate until further use. These treats can last for about 15 days.

APPLE AND CARROT COOKIES

Quantity Produced: 70 cookies	**Nutritional Values:** 1 cookie
Preparation Time: 20 minutes	*Calories:* 46
Cooking Time: 7 minutes	*Fat:* 2 g
	Carbohydrates: 5 g
	Protein: 2 g

Ingredients:

- 2 cups quick cooking or old-fashioned oats, coarsely powdered

- 2 teaspoons baking powder

- 2 cups all-purpose flour

- ½ cup shredded carrot

- ½ cup shredded apple

- ½ cup milk

- 1 cup creamy peanut butter

- 2 eggs

Directions:

1. Preheat the oven to 350 °F. Place the baking mat on a baking sheet with the flat side on top.

2. Add flour, baking soda, and oats into the mixing bowl of the stand mixer and mix until well combined.

3. Mix in the carrot and apple. Add milk, peanut butter, and eggs and mix until dough is formed.

4. Divide the dough into 70 equal parts and shape into cookies. Place as many as can fit on the baking mat. Bake the remaining in batches.

5. Bake for five minutes. Turn each cookie over and bake for another two minutes. Let them cool for a few minutes on the baking mat. Transfer onto a rack to cool completely.

6. Transfer into an airtight container and refrigerate until use. These treats can last for about two weeks. To make them last longer, freeze them. They can last for about three months.

BANANA BREAD SOFT CHEW DOG TREAT

Quantity Produced: About 6 ounces	**Nutritional Values:** Entire batch
Preparation Time: 10 minutes	*Calories:* 374
Cooking Time: 10-15 minutes	*Fat:* 28 g
	Carbohydrates: 22 g
	Protein: 13.5 g

Ingredients:

- ¼ cup coconut flour

- ¼ cup pumpkin puree

- ½ very ripe banana, mashed

- ½ tablespoon ground flaxseeds

- 1 large egg

- ½ tablespoon coconut oil

Directions:

1. Preheat the oven to 350 °F.

2. Place coconut flour and ground flax seeds in a bowl and stir well.

3. Add egg, pumpkin puree, banana, and coconut oil into another bowl and whisk until smooth. Add the flour mixture and whisk until smooth. The batter should be thick, like pancake batter.

4. Place the baking mat upturned on a baking sheet, with the cavity side up.

5. Fill the cavities with the batter.

6. Make sure the edges around the cavities are free from the batter. Lift the baking sheet and tap it lightly on your countertop to remove any air pockets. Bake in batches if required.

7. Bake in a preheated oven for about 20–25 minutes.

8. Let it cool for a while in the oven.

9. Cool completely on the countertop. Hold the baking mat on opposite edges and twist the baking sheet to unmold. Invert onto a baking sheet when completely cooled.

10. They can last for about seven days in the refrigerator in an airtight container.

BLUEBERRY, OATS, AND PEANUT BUTTER TREATS

Quantity Produced: 17 treats **Preparation Time:** 10 minutes **Cooking Time:** 40 minutes	**Nutritional Values:** 1 treat *Calories:* 50 *Fat:* 1 g *Carbohydrates:* 8 g *Protein:* 2 g

Ingredients:

- ½ cup fresh or frozen or dried blueberries

- 1 ¼ cups whole-wheat flour

- 1 ½ tablespoons peanut butter

- 2–4 tablespoons warm water or as required

- 6 tablespoons oats

- 1 egg

- ¼ teaspoon ground cinnamon

- ¼ teaspoon human-grade bone meal (optional)

- ¼ teaspoon organic kelp flakes (optional)

- ⅛ teaspoon kosher salt (optional)

- ¼ teaspoon turmeric powder

Directions:

1. Preheat the oven to 350 °F.

2. For the blueberries, if you want to use fresh or dried blueberries, chop them into smaller pieces. For the frozen blueberries, mash the berries.

3. Combine blueberries and oats in a bowl. Stir in egg, peanut butter, and salt. Stir in optional ingredients if using wheat flour and cinnamon. You will get a crumbly mixture.

4. Add 2 tablespoons of warm water at a time and mix well until dough is formed.

5. Place the baking mat on a baking sheet with the flat side on top.

6. Dust some flour on your countertop and place your dough on it.

7. Roll the dough with a rolling pin until it is about ½ inch thick.

8. Cut the rolled dough into treats using a bone-shaped cookie cutter or the desired shape. Gather the scrap dough and re-shape it into the dough. Repeat the rolling and cutting process until all the dough is used up. You should have 17 treats.

9. Place the treats on the baking mat.

10. Bake until firm; it should take around 40 minutes. Cool completely.

11. Transfer into an airtight container. These treats can last for about 15 days if stored in the refrigerator.

CRANBERRY COOKIES

Quantity Produced:	**Nutritional Values:** Entire Recipe
About 4–5 ounces	**Calories:** 495
	Fat: 18 g
Preparation Time: 15 minutes	**Carbohydrates:** 70 g
Cooking Time: 18 minutes	**Protein:** 19.5 g

Ingredients:

- 1 egg, beaten

- ½ tablespoon coconut oil

- ¼ cup dried cranberries

- ¾ cup whole-wheat flour

- 2 tablespoons coconut flour

Directions:

1. Preheat the oven to 325 °F. Place the baking mat on a baking sheet with the flat side on top.

2. Combine wheat flour, cranberries, and oil in a mixing bowl.

3. Add egg and mix with your hand until dough is formed.

4. Add a little coconut flour and mix well each time until well combined.

5. Dust your countertop with a little flour. Place the dough on your countertop.

6. Roll the dough with a rolling pin until it is about ⅓–½ inch thick.

7. Cut the rolled dough into treats using a bone-shaped cookie cutter or the desired shape. Gather the scrap dough and re-shape it into a dough. Repeat this process of rolling and cutting until all the dough is used up. You should have 17 treats.

8. Place the treats on the baking mat.

9. Bake for about 18 minutes or until crisp. Cool completely.

10. Transfer into an airtight container. These treats can last for about a week if stored in the refrigerator.

🐕 MILK COOKIES

Quantity Produced: 24 **Preparation Time:** 20 minutes **Cooking Time:** 30 minutes	**Nutritional Values:** 2 cookies *Calories:* 417 *Fat:* 20 g *Carbohydrates:* 49 g *Protein:* 14 g

Ingredients:

- 5 cups whole-wheat flour
- 1 ½ cups nonfat dry milk powder
- 1 ½ cups boiling water
- 4 tablespoons brown sugar
- 2 eggs, beaten
- 1 cup vegetable oil
- 4 beef bouillon cubes

Directions:

1. Preheat the oven to 300 °F.

2. Place a baking mat on a baking sheet with the flat side on top.

3. Add the bouillon cubes to the boiling water.

4. While it cools, add milk powder, flour, brown sugar, beef broth, oil, and eggs into a mixing bowl until well combined and dough is formed.

5. Knead the dough for a minute and place it on your countertop, which is dusted with some flour.

6. Roll the dough until it is ¼ inch thick.

7. Cut the rolled dough into treats using a bone-shaped cookie cutter or the desired shape. Gather the scrap dough and re-shape it into a dough. Repeat this process of rolling and cutting until all the dough is used up. You should have 24 treats.

8. Place the treats on the baking mat.

9. Bake until firm; it should take about 30 minutes. Allow it to cool completely.

10. Transfer into an airtight container. These treats can last for about a week in the refrigerator. They can last for about two months if you freeze them.

VEGAN DOG TREATS

Quantity Produced: 20	**Nutritional Values:** 1 treat
Preparation Time: 15 minutes	*Calories:* 28
Cooking Time: 30 minutes	*Fat:* 1.2 g
	Carbohydrates: 3.6 g
	Protein: 1 g

Ingredients:

- 6 tablespoons pumpkin puree

- 1 tablespoon ground flax seeds

- ¼ teaspoon ground cinnamon (optional)

- 2 tablespoons peanut butter

- ⅔ cup oat flour

Directions:

1. Preheat the oven to 350 °F. Place a baking mat on a baking sheet with the flat side facing up.

2. Blend peanut butter, pumpkin puree, cinnamon, and flax seeds in a food processor until well incorporated.

3. Mix in the oat flour. Mix until dough is formed.

4. Dust some flour on your countertop and place your dough on it.

5. Roll it with a rolling pin into a ¼ inch thick sheet.

6. Cut the rolled dough into treats using a cookie cutter of the desired shape. Gather the scrap dough and re-shape it into a dough. Repeat this process of rolling and cutting until all the dough is used up. You should have 20 treats.

7. Place the treats on the prepared baking mat.

8. Bake for 30 minutes and then cool it completely.

9. Store in an airtight container. These treats can last for about a week in the refrigerator. They can last for about two months if you freeze them.

CHICKEN DOG TREATS

Quantity Produced: 24	**Nutritional Values:** 1 treat
Preparation Time: 10 minutes	*Calories:* 33
Cooking Time: 12-14 minutes	*Fat:* 1 g
	Carbohydrates: 4 g
	Protein: 2 g

Ingredients:

- 1 cup cooked, chopped chicken (any leftover chicken works)

- 1 small egg, beaten

- 6 tablespoons water

- 2.6 ounces of nonfat plain Greek yogurt

- 1 cup whole-wheat flour or white whole-wheat flour

Directions:

1. Preheat the oven to 350 °F. Place a baking mat on a baking sheet with the flat side on top.

2. Add chicken, yogurt, egg, flour, and water into a bowl and mix until well combined. You will get sticky batter which will be thick as well.

3. Line a baking sheet with parchment paper. Scoop a tablespoonful of batter and drop it on the baking sheet, leaving sufficient space between the cookies. You should get 24 treats in all.

4. Now flatten the dough a little. You can use the back of a spoon to do so. Place the baking sheet in the oven until they turn light golden brown.

5. Cool the treats for a few minutes on the mat and then transfer them onto a wire rack to cool. Store the cookies in an airtight container; they can last for about a week in the refrigerator. They can last for about two months in the freezer.

CANINE COOKIES

Quantity Produced: 30 **Preparation Time:** 15 minutes **Cooking Time:** 30 minutes	**Nutritional Values:** 1 cookie without cranberries *Calories:* 16 *Fat:* 0.35 g *Carbohydrates:* 2.6 g *Protein:* 0.6 g

Ingredients:

- 1 cup cooked, mashed sweet potato
- ¼ teaspoon ground cinnamon
- ¼ teaspoon ground ginger
- 1 cup finely grated carrots
- ½ cup finely diced apple
- 30 dried cranberries (optional)
- 2 large eggs

Directions:

1. Preheat your oven to 350 °F.

2. Combine sweet potato, carrot, apple, cinnamon, ginger, and eggs in a bowl.

3. Place a baking mat over a baking sheet.

4. Make 30 equal portions (about 1 ½–2 teaspoons per cookie) of the mixture. Shape each portion into a ball. Flatten the cookie to the desired thickness and place it on the mat, leaving a gap between them. Place a cranberry on the center of each cookie and press it slightly into the cookie.

5. Bake in a preheated oven for 30 minutes.

6. Allow them to cool for a few minutes on the baking sheet, and then shift them onto a wire rack to cool.

7. Transfer the cookies to an airtight container and place them in the refrigerator. Use within four days. They can last for about a month if frozen.

PUMPKIN APPLE TREATS

Quantity Produced: 80 **Preparation Time:** 25 -30 minutes **Cooking Time:** 35 minutes	**Nutritional Values:** 1 treat *Calories:* 50 *Fat:* 1.2 g *Carbohydrates:* 8.6 g *Protein:* 1.9 g

Ingredients:

- 1 cup oatmeal (grind oats until finely powdered)

- 6 cups whole-wheat flour

- 2 large apples, cored, peeled, finely chopped

- 1 cup pumpkin puree, unsweetened

- 1 cup cold water

- 2 eggs

- 4 tablespoons brown sugar

Directions:

1. Preheat the oven to 350 °F. Place a large baking mat on a large baking sheet.

2. Add flour and oatmeal into a mixing bowl and stir.

3. Add apples, pumpkin puree, water, eggs, and brown sugar and mix until dough is formed.

4. Dust your countertop with a little flour. Place the dough on your countertop and knead the dough for a couple of minutes. Make 80 equal portions of the dough and shape it into balls. Flatten each until it is ¼ inch thick.

5. You can also give the shape of your choice.

6. Place treats on the baking mat, in a single layer, without overlapping. Place as many as can fit.

7. Bake in batches for 35 minutes or until the edges turn brown. Switch off the oven. Let the cookies cool in the oven for about 45 minutes.

8. Cool the cookies completely on your countertop.

9. Transfer the cookies to an airtight container and place them in the refrigerator. Use within two weeks. You can also freeze them for about two months.

SWEET POTATO DOG TREATS

Quantity Produced: 16 **Preparation Time:** 15 minutes **Cooking Time:** 35 minutes	**Nutritional Values:** 1 cookie *Calories:* 43 *Fat:* 1 g *Carbohydrates:* 9.9 g *Protein:* 2 g

Ingredients:

- ½ sweet potato

- 1 large egg

- 1 ¼ cups whole-wheat flour

- 2 tablespoons unsweetened applesauce

Directions:

1. Preheat your oven to 350 °F.

2. Take a sweet potato and pierce the sweet potato at a few places with a knife. Place it in the microwave and cook on high for about five minutes or until soft.

3. When it cools, peel and mash the sweet potato. You need ½ cup of mashed sweet potato, so choose the sweet potato accordingly before cooking. You can use the remaining sweet potato in some other recipes.

4. Add sweet potato, flour, applesauce, and egg into a bowl and mix until dough is formed.

5. Dust your countertop with a little flour. Place the dough on your countertop and roll with a rolling pin until the dough is about ½ inch thick.

6. You can cut the dough into strips or cut it with a cookie cutter. A bone-shaped one will work.

7. You should have 16 treats in all.

8. Place the cookies on a baking mat placed over a baking sheet.

9. Place it in the oven to bake until crisp. It should take around 35–45 minutes.

10. Let them cool for a few minutes on the baking mat. Transfer the cookies onto a wire rack to cool to room temperature.

11. Transfer the cookies to an airtight container and place them in the refrigerator. Use within four days. They can last for about a month if frozen.

SPINACH, CARROT, AND ZUCCHINI DOG TREATS

Quantity Produced: About 12–14 ounces **Preparation Time:** 25 minutes **Cooking Time:** 25 minutes	**Nutritional Values:** Entire recipe *Calories:* 1279 *Fat:* 43.5 g *Carbohydrates:* 182 g *Protein:* 52.9 g

Ingredients:

- ½ cup pumpkin puree

- 1 large egg

- 1 ½ cups whole-wheat flour or more if required

- ½ carrot, peeled, shredded

- ½ cup baby spinach, chopped

- ½ zucchini, shredded

- 2 tablespoons peanut butter

- ¼ cup old-fashioned oats

Directions:

1. Preheat your oven to 350 °F. Place a baking mat on a baking sheet.

2. Fix the electric hand mixer or stand mixer with the paddle attachment.

3. Add pumpkin puree, egg, and peanut butter into the mixing bowl and beat for a few minutes.

4. Add 1 ¼ cups of flour and oats and beat until just combined. Add remaining flour, 2 tablespoons at a time, and mix well each time until well combined.

5. Beat in the zucchini, carrot, and spinach.

6. Dust your countertop with a little flour. Place the dough on your countertop and knead the dough for a couple of minutes. Roll the dough with a rolling pin until it is ¼ inch thick. You can cut into treats using a pizza cutter into sticks or cut into shapes with a cookie cutter.

7. Place treats on the baking mat, in a single layer, without overlapping.

8. Bake for 20–25 minutes or until the edges turn brown.

9. Cool the cookies for a few minutes on the baking mat. Transfer onto a rack to cool completely.

10. Transfer the cookies to an airtight container and place them in the refrigerator. Use within two weeks. You can also freeze them for about two months.

VANILLA YOGURT COOKIES

Quantity Produced:	Nutritional Values: Entire batch
About 12–15 ounces	*Calories:* 1110
	Fat: 5.4 g
Preparation Time: 10 minutes	*Carbohydrates:* 233.8 g
Cooking Time: 10 minutes	*Protein:* 27.6 g

Ingredients:

- 1 ½ cups white rice flour

- ½ cup plain full-fat yogurt

- 2 tablespoons honey

- 2 egg whites, beaten

- ¼ teaspoon vanilla extract

Directions:

1. Preheat the oven to 350 °F. Place the baking mat on a baking sheet with the flat side on top.

2. Add whites, honey, vanilla, and yogurt into a bowl and whisk until smooth.

3. Add flour and mix until dough is formed.

4. Dust your countertop with a bit of flour. Place the dough on your countertop.

5. Roll the dough with a rolling pin until it is about ¼ inch thick.

6. Cut the rolled dough into cookies using a round cookie cutter or the desired shape. Gather the scrap dough and re-shape it into a dough. Repeat this rolling and cutting process until all the dough is used up.

7. Place the cookies on the baking mat.

8. Bake for about 10 minutes or until light brown. Cool completely.

9. Transfer into an airtight container and refrigerate until use. These cookies can last for about a week.

FENNEL DOG TREATS

Quantity Produced:	Nutritional Values: Entire batch
About 4–5 ounces	Calories: 656
	Fat: 6.5 g
Preparation Time: 10 minutes	Carbohydrates: 130.6 g
Cooking Time: 10 minutes	Protein: 15 g

Ingredients:

- 1 cup white rice flour
- ½ teaspoon carbonate calcium powder
- 2 tablespoons unsweetened applesauce
- ¼ teaspoon powdered fennel
- 1 egg

Directions:

1. Preheat the oven to 325 °F. Place the baking mat on a baking sheet with the flat side on top. Add rice flour, fennel, carbonate calcium powder, egg, and applesauce into a bowl and mix until a smooth dough is formed.

2. Dust your countertop with a bit of flour. Place the dough on your countertop. Roll the dough with a rolling pin until it is about ¼ inch thick.

3. Cut the rolled dough into cookies using a round cookie cutter or the desired shape. Gather the scrap dough and re-shape it into a dough. Repeat this rolling and cutting process until all the dough is used up.

4. Place the cookies on the baking mat. Bake for about 10 minutes or until light brown. Cool completely.

5. Transfer into an airtight container and refrigerate until use. These cookies can last for about a week.

🐕 DOGGIE BREATH MINTS

Quantity Produced: 20	**Nutritional Values:** 1 breath mint
Preparation Time: 20 minutes	*Calories:* 30
Cooking Time: 40 minutes	*Fat:* 1 g
	Carbohydrates: 4 g
	Protein: 1g

Ingredients:

- 1 ¼ cups old-fashioned oats, ground into fine powder

- ¼ cup fresh mint leaves, finely chopped

- 2 ½ tablespoons water

- ¼ cup fresh parsley leaves, finely chopped

- 1 small egg or 2 tablespoons unsweetened applesauce

- 1 ½ tablespoons melted coconut oil

Directions:

1. Preheat the oven to 350 °F. Place a sheet of baking mat on a large baking sheet.

2. Crack the egg into a bowl. Add oil and water and whisk until well combined. Add mint and parsley leaves and whisk well.

3. Stir in the oat flour. Mix until dough is formed. Knead for about a minute.

4. Dust your countertop with a little flour. Place the dough on your countertop and knead the dough for a couple of minutes. Roll the dough with a rolling pin until it is ⅛ inch thick. Cut into 20 equal portions using a knife. You can also use a cookie cutter of bone or desired shape to cut the cookies. If you are using a cookie cutter, collect the scrap dough and re-shape it after you cut the cookies. Repeat this step until all the dough is used up. You should have 20 cookies in all.

5. Place treats on the baking mat, in a single layer, without overlapping.

6. Bake for 35–40 minutes or until they turn golden brown. You can serve the cookies warm.

7. Cool the leftover cookies completely before transferring them into an airtight container and then place them in the refrigerator. Use within two weeks. You can also freeze them for about two months.

CHAPTER 9:

COOKIES AND TREATS FOR DOGS WITH HEALTH ISSUES

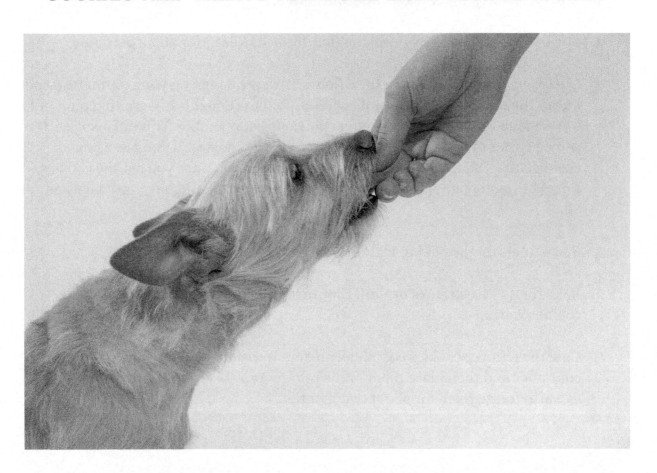

🐕 APPLE PEANUT BUTTER TREATS FOR DIABETIC DOGS

Quantity Produced: 6 large treats	**Nutritional Values:** 1 treat
Preparation Time: 10 minutes	*Calories:* 220
Cooking Time: 20 -25 minutes	*Fat: 8 g*
	Carbohydrates: 9.3 g
	Protein: 9.3g

7

Ingredients:

- 2 cups oat flour or more if required

- ¼ cup natural peanut butter

- ⅓ cup unsweetened applesauce

- 1 large egg

Directions:

1. Preheat the oven to 350 °F. Place a baking mat on a large baking sheet.

2. Crack the egg into a bowl. Add applesauce and peanut butter and whisk until smooth.

3. Stir in the oat flour. Mix until dough is formed. If the dough is very sticky, add some extra oat flour, a tablespoon at a time, and mix well each time until it is not sticky anymore.

4. Dust your countertop with a little flour. Place the dough on your countertop and knead the dough for a couple of minutes. Roll the dough with a rolling pin until it is ¼ inch thick.

5. Using a large cookie cutter, cut the cookies. Collect the scrap dough and re-roll it into a ball. Repeat step 4 until all the dough is used up.

6. Place the cookies on the baking mat in the oven for baking with the timer set for about 20–25 minutes or until the edges are brown.

1. Cool the cookies for a few minutes on the baking mat. Transfer onto a rack to cool completely.

2. Transfer the cookies to an airtight container and place them in the refrigerator. Use within two weeks. You can also freeze them for about three months.

DOG TREATS FOR SENSITIVE STOMACH

Quantity Produced: 36 **Preparation Time:** 5 minutes **Cooking Time:** 20 minutes	**Nutritional Values:** 1 treat *Calories:* 19 *Fat:* 0.4 g *Carbohydrates:* 3 g *Protein:* 0.8g

Ingredients:

- 1 ½ cups old-fashioned rolled oats

- 1 large egg

- ½ cup pumpkin puree

Directions:

1. Preheat the oven to 350 °F. Place a baking mat on a large baking sheet with the flat side on top.

2. Add egg and pumpkin puree into a bowl and whisk until smooth. Add oats and mix until dough is formed.

3. Make 36 equal portions of the dough (about a tablespoon per portion).

4. Place the cookies on the baking mat. Place it in the oven and bake until golden brown, about 20 minutes.

5. Cool the cookies for a few minutes on the baking mat. Transfer the cookies onto a rack. Let them cool completely.

6. Transfer the cookies to an airtight container and place them in the refrigerator. Use within two weeks. You can also freeze them for about three months.

🐕 DOG TREAT FOR DOGS WITH KIDNEY DISEASE

Quantity Produced: 9 treats **Preparation Time:** 15 minutes **Cooking Time:** 25 minutes	**Nutritional Values:** 1 treat *Calories:* 57 *Fat:* 0.4 g *Carbohydrates:* 12.1 g *Protein:* 2.2g

Ingredients:

- 1 ¼ cups whole-wheat flour

- ¼ cup cold water

- 3 tablespoons low-sodium, low-fat chicken broth

- ½ cup cooked vegetables of your choice, pureed

Directions:

1. Preheat the oven to 350 °F. Place a baking mat on a baking sheet with the flat side on top.

2. Add flour into a mixing bowl. Add chicken broth and vegetables and stir. Stir in cold water. Mix until dough is formed.

3. Dust your countertop with a little flour. Place the dough on your countertop and knead the dough for a couple of minutes. Roll the dough with a rolling pin until it is ½ inch thick.

4. Using a cookie cutter, cut the cookies. Collect the scrap dough and re-roll it into a ball. Repeat step four until all the dough is used up.

5. Place the cookies on the baking mat and place them in the oven for baking with the timer set for about 20–25 minutes or until the edges are brown.

6. Cool the cookies for a few minutes on the baking mat. Transfer onto a rack to cool completely.

7. Transfer the cookies to an airtight container and place them in the refrigerator. Use within two weeks. You can also freeze them for about three months.

🐕 BANANA ALMOND DOG TREATS

Quantity Produced: 25 treats **Preparation Time:** 15 minutes **Cooking Time:** 20 minutes	**Nutritional Values:** 1 treat *Calories:* 15 *Fat:* 1 g *Carbohydrates:* 1.2 g *Protein:* 0.9g

Ingredients:

- ⅛ cup almond flour

- ¾ cup coconut flour

- 3 tablespoons almond butter or peanut butter

- 1 large egg

- ½ tablespoon melted coconut oil

- ¼ cup mashed overripe banana

- ½ tablespoon maple syrup

- 2 tablespoons almond milk or any milk of your choice

Directions:

1. Preheat the oven to 300 °F.

2. Place a silicone mold with a paw print shape on a baking sheet.

3. Combine almond flour and coconut flour in a mixing bowl. Yes, I know almonds come under forbidden foods. You can give a little of it to your dog and see if it

suits him. My dog had a gluten allergy, so I made these treats for him. He was ok with it. You can also replace almond flour with peanut flour if desired and use any other milk of your choice instead of almond milk.

4. Whisk together egg, peanut butter, maple syrup, oil, and banana until smooth.

5. Stir the flour mixture into the bowl of egg mixture, a little at a time, and stir well each time.

6. Mix in the milk, using your hands, until you get a soft dough. It will crumble slightly.

7. Fill the dough into the molds. Fill as many cavities as possible on your mold and bake the remaining in batches.

8. Bake for about 20 minutes or until firm. Let the treats cool in the molds for 10 minutes. Unmold and cool on a wire rack. Store completely cooled treats in an airtight container. Place them in the refrigerator, which will last about two weeks.

CONCLUSION

With this book, you can make all sorts of tasty treats for your dog. Always practice good hygiene while making, baking, or handling the treats to avoid bacteria or mold. When trying out new recipes, check the list of foods that should be avoided so you don't feed them something harmful. The list given in this book should be helpful for this.

To safely store dog treats, keep the ingredients and environmental conditions in mind. Heat, light, and moisture are factors that will reduce shelf life. Keeping the food in cool, dark places in airtight containers or bags will keep it from spoiling.

Your pet might have some special dietary requirements, so keep them in mind and adjust the recipes as needed. You can also ask your vet for advice on what your dog should or shouldn't eat. In general, make treats using natural and healthy ingredients that will provide your dog with nutrients. Avoid giving them any junk food or anything with sugar. Any fruit high in natural sugars should also be given in moderation.

Another tip is to avoid adding too many nuts to your dog's diet if they are overweight. The high-fat content can lead to obesity. It may be tempting to spoil your dog with treats all the time, but moderation is key. Treats should be given in small amounts and should not be given excessively. However, with the healthy recipes given in this book, you can give your dog delicious treats without too much concern. I hope you enjoy trying these baking mat recipes!

REFERENCES

Dalmatian DIY. (2019, September 24). *Homemade baked dog treat shelf life and storage.* Dalmatian DIY. https://www.dalmatiandiy.com/shelf-life-and-storage-for-baked-dog-treats/

How To Store Homemade Dog Treats. (n.d.). Wiggleworthy https://www.wiggleworthy.com/store-homemade-dog-treats.html#:~:text=Homemade%20dog%20

Seven Baked Dog Treat Recipes for our Fluffy Friends! (n.d.). Cotswold Flour. https://cotswoldflour.com/blogs/baking-resources/7-baked-dog-treat-recipes-for-our-fluffy-friends

Walther, R. (2021, May 21). *List of food dogs can (and can't) eat, according to vet.* Pawlicy Advisor. https://www.pawlicy.com/blog/food-dogs-can-and-cant-eat/

IMAGE REFERENCES

Coulton, M. (2020, May 15). Commercial dog food. *Pixabay.* https://pixabay.com/photos/dog-food-dog-bowl-dog-kibble-5168940/

Glazer, S. (2016, July 7). Dog eating. *Pixabay.* https://pixabay.com/photos/puppy-bone-dog-pet-animal-food-1502565/

katerinavulcova. (2020, February 18). Storing dog food. *Pixabay.* https://pixabay.com/photos/dog-treats-trade-shopping-goods-3162326/

Ozsvath, C. (2021, October 14). Healthy dog. *Pixabay.* https://pixabay.com/photos/corgi-dog-pet-pembroke-welsh-corgi-6705821/

Martine. (2015, July 14). Dog treat. *Pixabay.* https://pixabay.com/photos/dog-eat-biscuit-reward-843800/

Parkinson, J. (2021, December 15). Dog biscuit. Pixabay. https://pixabay.com/photos/dog-treats-bone-biscuit-dog-food-6870910/

StockSnap. (2017, August 4). Dog treat. *Pixabay.* https://pixabay.com/photos/dog-puppy-animal-cute-pet-clothes-2583282/

tpiety. (2015, July 6). Pumpkin Dog treat. *Pixabay.* https://pixabay.com/photos/halloween-cookie-dog-treat-832285/

Tri Tam , T. M. (2016, January 27). Happy dog. *Pixabay.* https://pixabay.com/photos/girl-lady-woman-women-asia-female-1160441/

Yuriko Smith, A. (2019, November 20). Dog treat. *Pixabay.* https://pixabay.com/photos/biscuit-dog-treat-snack-bone-food-4638412/